Which Has More?

Name
Date

■ Which has more liquid? Circle the container that is holding more liquid.

①

②

③

④

1

■Which has more liquid? Circle the container that is holding more liquid.

①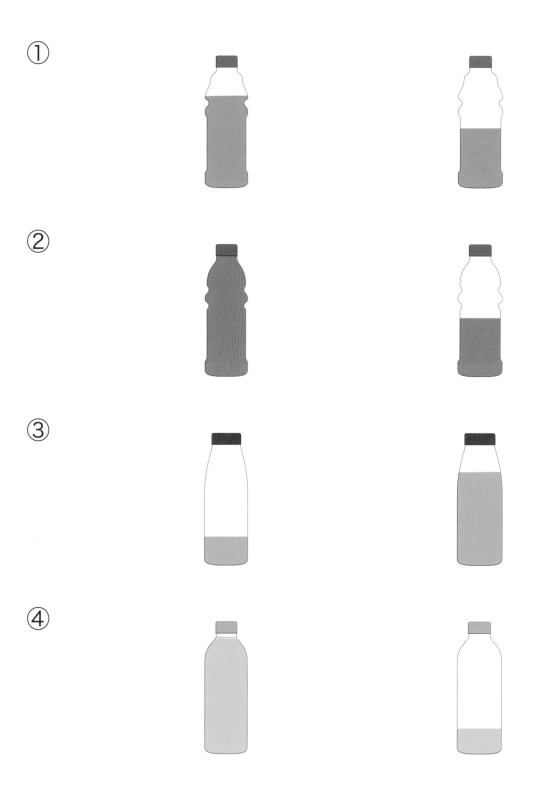

②

③

④

Which Has Less?

■ Which has less liquid? Circle the container that is holding less liquid.

①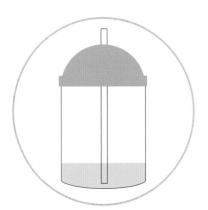

②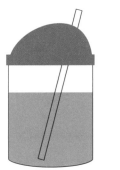

③  (right container)

④

■ Which has less liquid? Circle the container that is holding less liquid.

①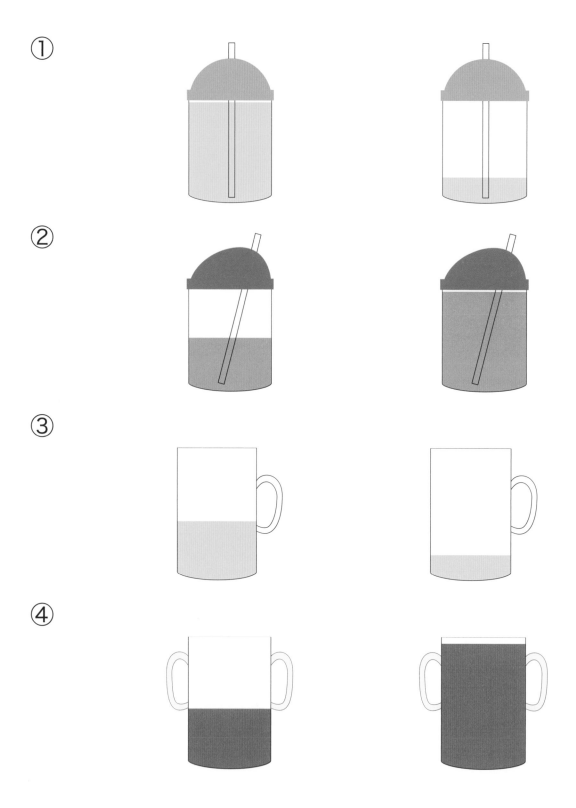

②

③

④

3 Most and Least

Name

Date

■ Which has the most liquid, and which has the least? Write a check
(✔) under the cup with the most liquid and a circle (○) under the
cup with the least liquid.

①

(○)   (   )   (✔)

②

(   )   (   )   (   )

③

(   )   (   )   (   )

④

(   )   (   )   (   )

■Which has the most liquid, and which has the least? Write a check
(✔) under the cup with the most liquid and a circle (○) under the
cup with the least liquid.

①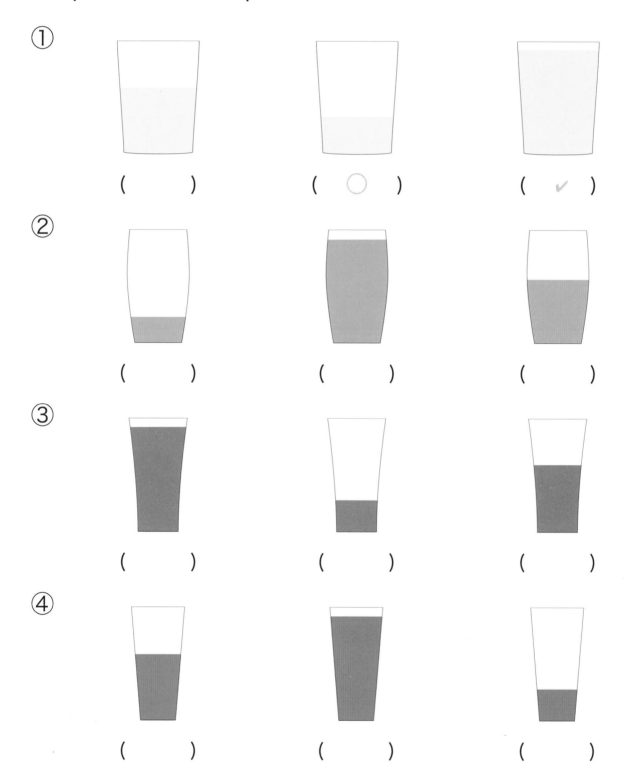

①
(   )   (○)   (✔)

②
(   )   (   )   (   )

③
(   )   (   )   (   )

④
(   )   (   )   (   )

6

4 Most and Least

■ Which has the most liquid, and which has the least? Write a check (✔) under the bottle with the most liquid and a circle (○) under the bottle with the least liquid.

①

( )   ( )   ( )

②

( )   ( )   ( )

③

( )   ( )   ( )

④

( )   ( )   ( )

■Which has the most liquid, and which has the least? Write a check
  (✔) under the bottle with the most liquid and a circle (○) under the
  bottle with the least liquid.

①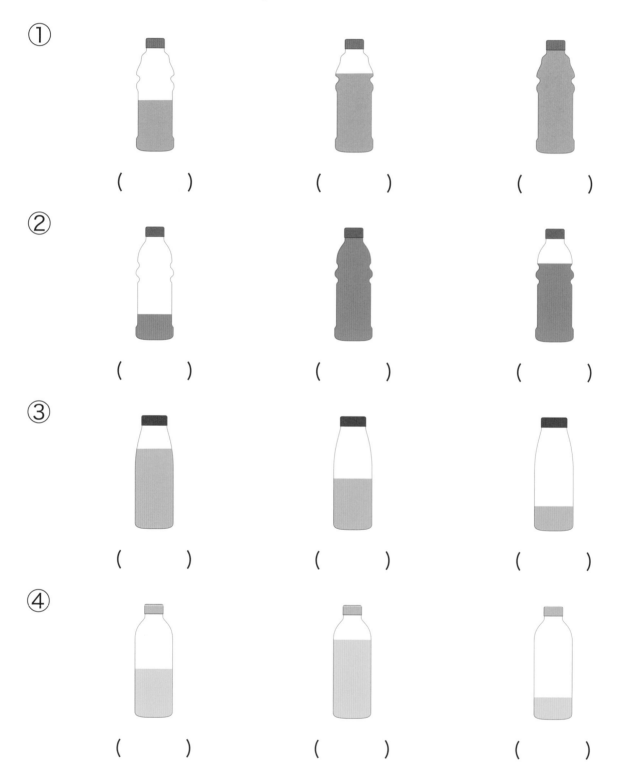

(   )   (   )   (   )

②

(   )   (   )   (   )

③

(   )   (   )   (   )

④

(   )   (   )   (   )

Most and Least

Name

Date

■ Which has the most liquid, and which has the least? Write a check
(✔) under the cup with the most liquid and a circle (○) under the
cup with the least liquid.

①

(   )   (   )   (   )

②

(   )   (   )   (   )

③

(   )   (   )   (   )

④

(   )   (   )   (   )

■Which has the most liquid, and which has the least? Write a check
(✔) under the cup with the most liquid and a circle (○) under the
cup with the least liquid.

①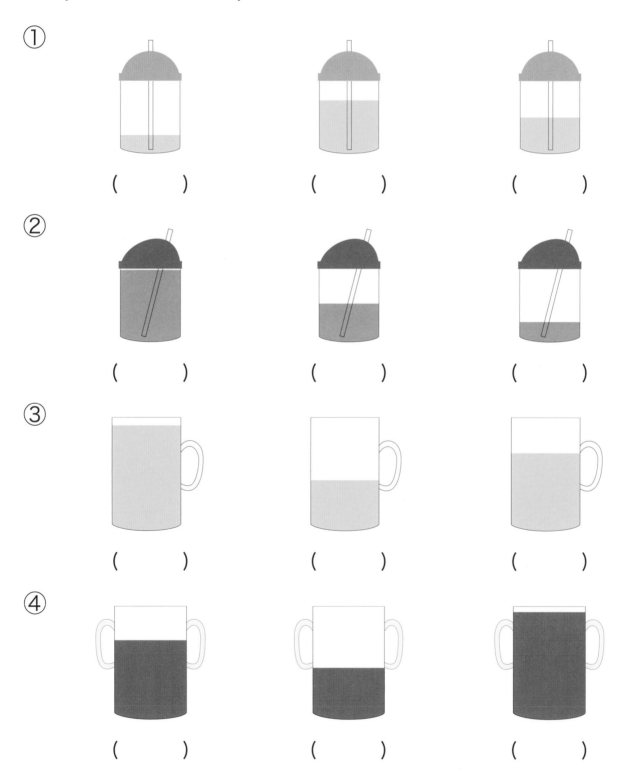

(   )   (   )   (   )

②

(   )   (   )   (   )

③

(   )   (   )   (   )

④

(   )   (   )   (   )

Equal Volume

Name

Date

■ Each cup below is the same size. Color in the liquid in the cup on the right side to match the volume of liquid in the cup on the left side.

①

②

③

④

■ Each cup below is the same size. Color in the liquid in the cup on the right side to match the volume of liquid in the cup on the left side.

①

②

③

④

 **Which Holds More?**

Name
Date

■ Which has more liquid? Circle the container that holds more cups of liquid.

①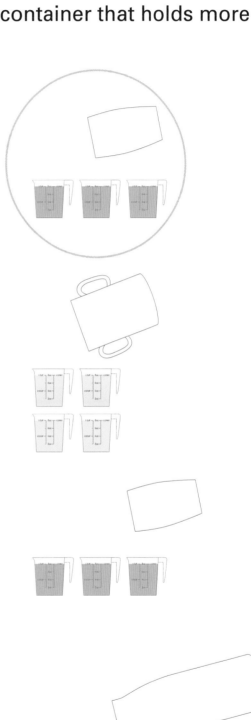

②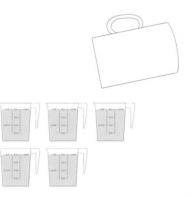

③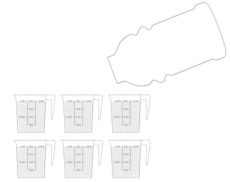

④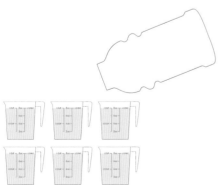

■Which has more liquid? Circle the container that holds more cups of liquid.

①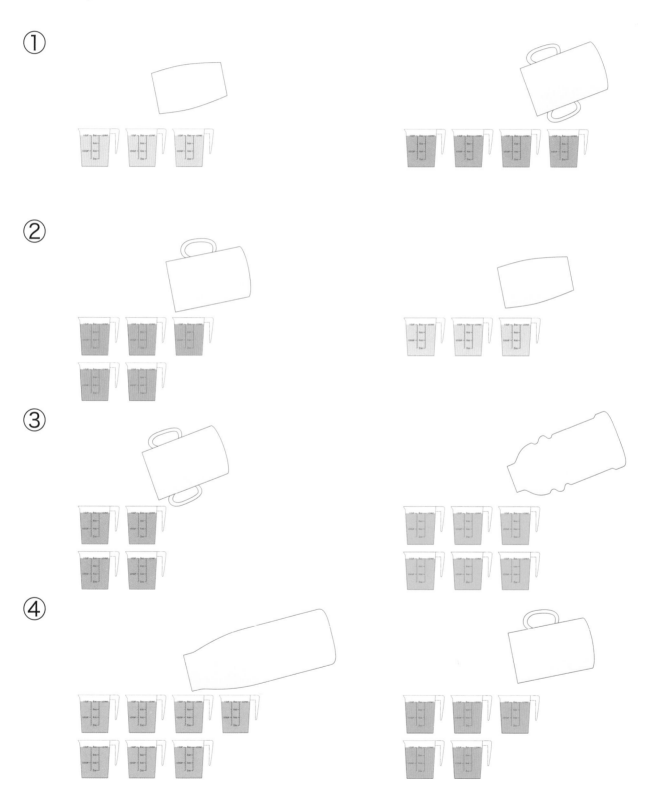

②

③

④

Which Holds More?

■ Which has more liquid? Circle the container that holds more cups of liquid.

①

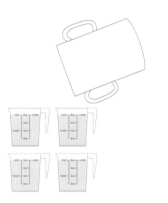 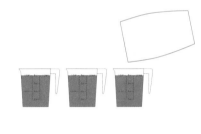

②

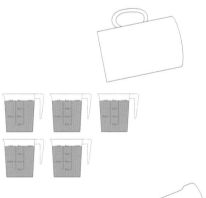 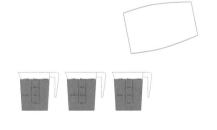

③

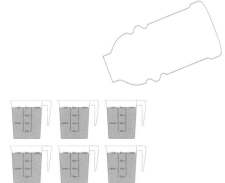

④

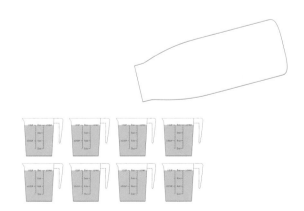

■Which has more liquid? Circle the container that holds more cups
   of liquid.

①

②

③

④

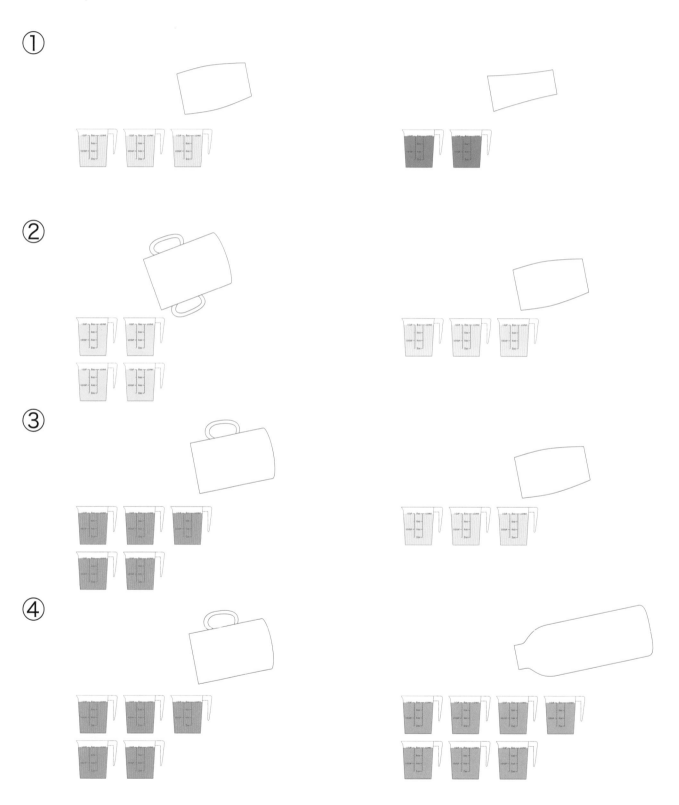

Which Holds More?

Name

Date

■ Which has more liquid? Circle the container that holds more cups of liquid.

①

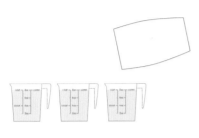

②

③

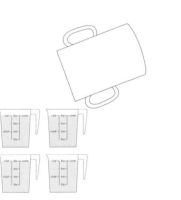

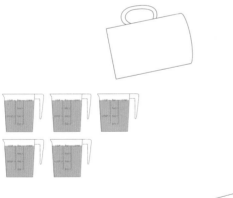

④

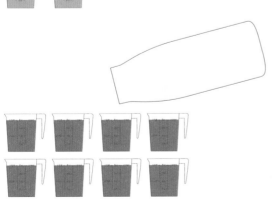

■Which has more liquid? Circle the container that holds more cups
  of liquid.

①

②

③

④

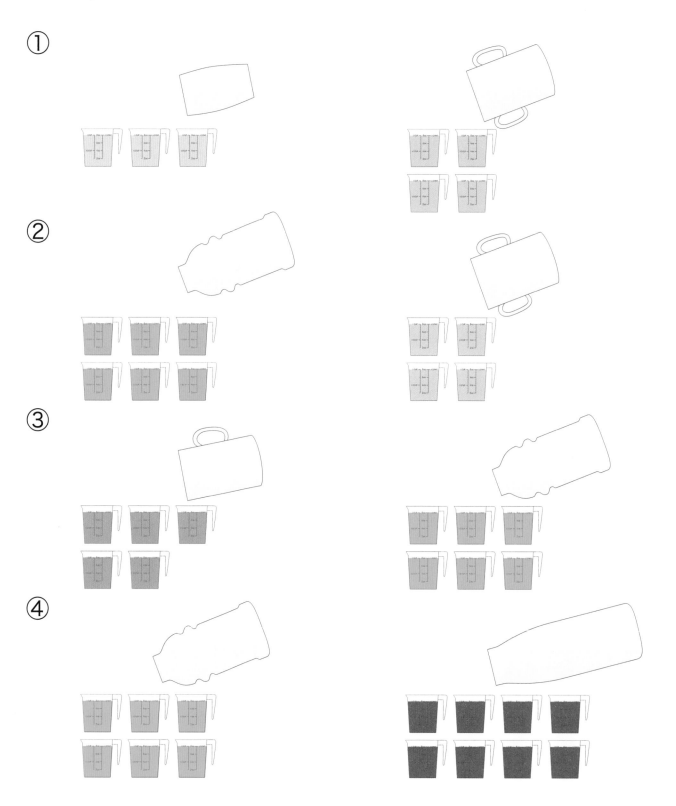

10 Most and Least

■ Which has the most liquid, and which has the least? Write a check
(✔) under the container with the most liquid and a circle (○) under
the container with the least liquid.

①

(　　　)　　　　　　　　(　　　)　　　　　　　　(　　　)

②

(　　　)　　　　　　　　(　　　)　　　　　　　　(　　　)

③

(　　　)　　　　　　　　(　　　)　　　　　　　　(　　　)

④

(　　　)　　　　　　　　(　　　)　　　　　　　　(　　　)

19

■Which has the most liquid, and which has the least? Write a check
(✔) under the container with the most liquid and a circle (○) under
the container with the least liquid.

①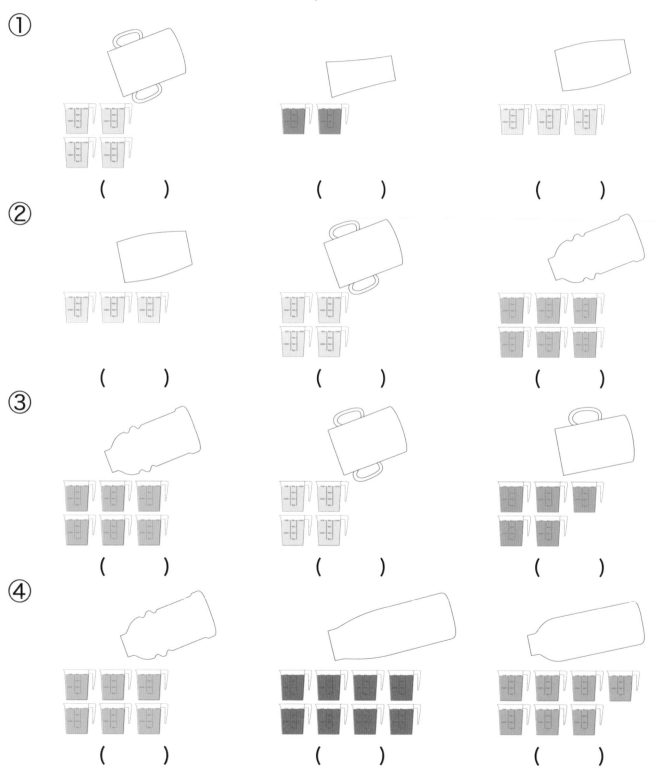

( )   ( )   ( )

②

( )   ( )   ( )

③

( )   ( )   ( )

④

( )   ( )   ( )

 **Most and Least**

Name

Date

■ Which has the most liquid, and which has the least? Write a check (✔) under the container with the most liquid and a circle (○) under the container with the least liquid.

①

(   )   (   )   (   )

②

(   )   (   )   (   )

③

(   )   (   )   (   )

④

(   )   (   )   (   )

■Which has the most liquid, and which has the least? Write a check
(✔) under the container with the most liquid and a circle (○) under
the container with the least liquid.

①

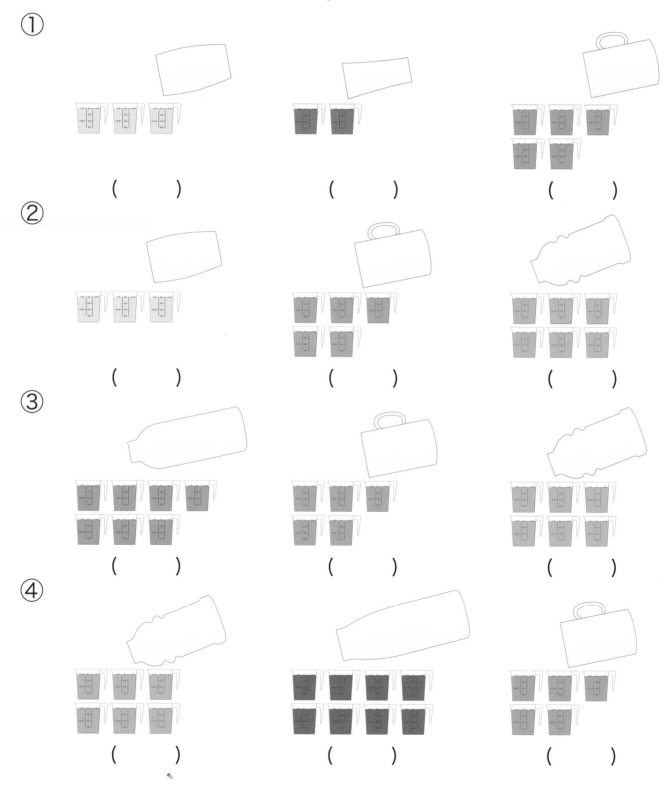

(   )   (   )   (   )

②

(   )   (   )   (   )

③

(   )   (   )   (   )

④

(   )   (   )   (   )

12 Equal Volume

■ Each measuring cup below is the same size. Color in the liquid in the measuring cups on the right side to match the volume of liquid in the measuring cups on the left side.

①

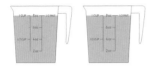
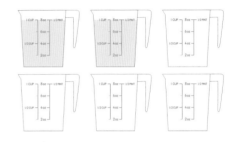

②

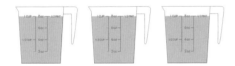

③

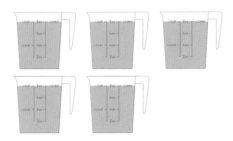
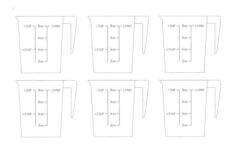

④

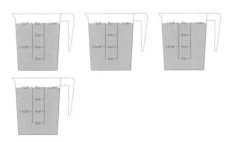

■Each measuring cup below is the same size. Color in the liquid in the measuring cups on the right side to match the volume of liquid in the measuring cups on the left side.

①

②

③

④

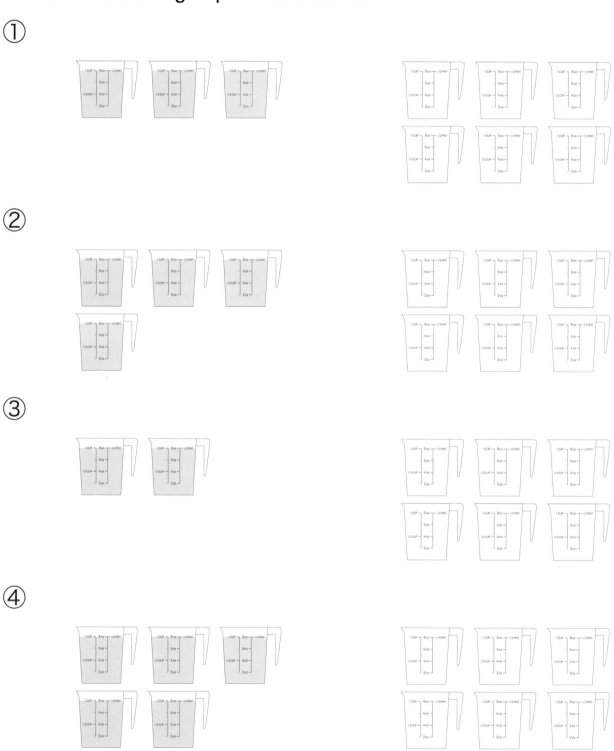

Name

Date

■ Which has the most liquid, and which has the least? Write a check (✔) under the cup with the most liquid and a circle (○) under the cup with the least liquid.

① (   )   (   )   (   )

② (   )   (   )   (   )

③ (   )   (   )   (   )

④ (   )   (   )   (   )

■Which has the most liquid, and which has the least? Write a check
 (✔) under the container with the most liquid and a circle (○) under
 the container with the least liquid.

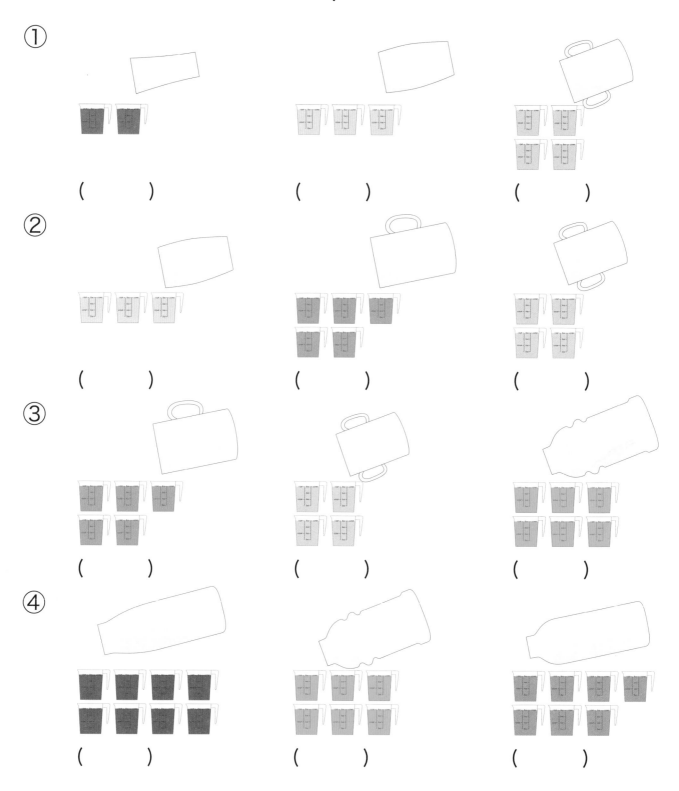

① ( ) ( ) ( )

② ( ) ( ) ( )

③ ( ) ( ) ( )

④ ( ) ( ) ( )

14 Practicing Numbers 1 to 100

Name

Date

■ Trace each number while saying it aloud.

1	2	3	4	5	6	7	8	9	10
11	12	13	14	15	16	17	18	19	20
21	22	23	24	25	26	27	28	29	30
31	32	33	34	35	36	37	38	39	40
41	42	43	44	45	46	47	48	49	50
51	52	53	54	55	56	57	58	59	60
61	62	63	64	65	66	67	68	69	70
71	72	73	74	75	76	77	78	79	80
81	82	83	84	85	86	87	88	89	90
91	92	93	94	95	96	97	98	99	100

■Trace each number while saying it aloud.

1	2	3	4	5	6	7	8	9	10
11	12	13	14	15	16	17	18	19	20
21	22	23	24	25	26	27	28	29	30
31	32	33	34	35	36	37	38	39	40
41	42	43	44	45	46	47	48	49	50
51	52	53	54	55	56	57	58	59	60
61	62	63	64	65	66	67	68	69	70
71	72	73	74	75	76	77	78	79	80
81	82	83	84	85	86	87	88	89	90
91	92	93	94	95	96	97	98	99	100

15 Practicing Numbers 1 to 100

Name

Date

■Trace each number while saying it aloud.

1	2	3	4	5	6	7	8	9	10
11	12	13	14	15	16	17	18	19	20
21	22	23	24	25	26	27	28	29	30
31	32	33	34	35	36	37	38	39	40
41	42	43	44	45	46	47	48	49	50
51	52	53	54	55	56	57	58	59	60
61	62	63	64	65	66	67	68	69	70
71	72	73	74	75	76	77	78	79	80
81	82	83	84	85	86	87	88	89	90
91	92	93	94	95	96	97	98	99	100

■ Write each number while saying it aloud.

1	2	3	4	5	6	7	8	9	10
11	12	13	14	15	16	17	18	19	20
21	22	23	24	25	26	27	28	29	30
31	32	33	34	35	36	37	38	39	40
41	42	43	44	45	46	47	48	49	50
51	52	53	54	55	56	57	58	59	60
61	62	63	64	65	66	67	68	69	70
71	72	73	74	75	76	77	78	79	80
81	82	83	84	85	86	87	88	89	90
91	92	93	94	95	96	97	98	99	100

16 Practicing Numbers 1 to 100

Name

Date

■ Write the missing number in each box.

1	2		4		6			9	
11		13	14			17		19	
	22	23		25			28		30
		33		35	36			39	
41			44			47		49	
	52		54	55		57	58		60
61		63		65	66			69	
	72		74			77		79	
81		83	84		86		88		90
	92	93		95		97			100

■Write the missing number in each box.

1		3		5		7		9	10
	12			15			18		
21		23	24			27		29	
31	32			35		37			40
	43		45	46			48	49	
	52		54			57			60
61	62			65	66		68		
71		73		75		77	78		
	82			85		87	88		90
91		93	94			97	98		100

32

17 Cups

Name	
Date	

■ Each measuring cup below equals 1 cup. Trace the number of cups of liquid in the space provided.

①

(1 cup)

②

(2 cups)

③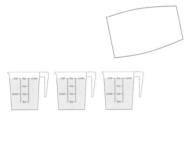

(3 cups)

④

(4 cups)

⑤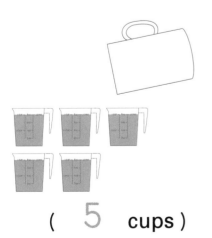

(5 cups)

■Each measuring cup below equals I cup. Write the number of cups
of liquid in the space provided.

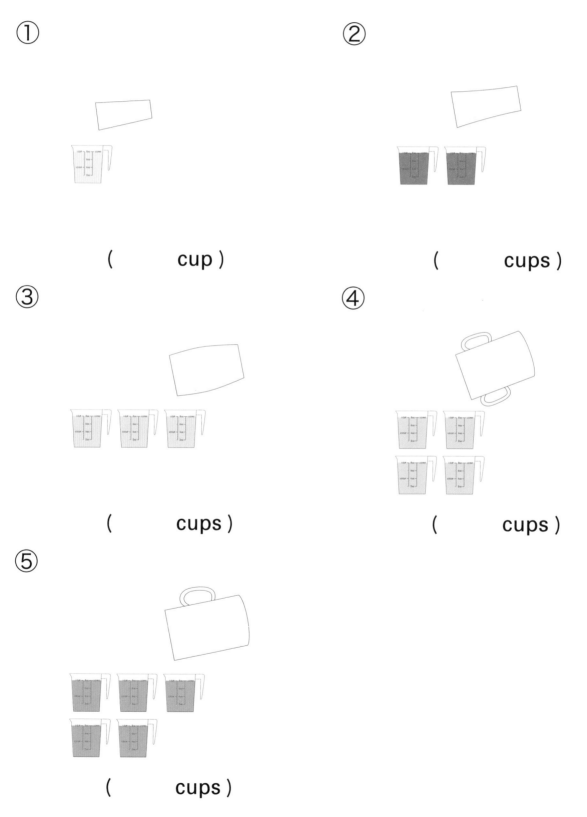

①

(cup)

②

(cups)

③

(cups)

④

(cups)

⑤

(cups)

Name

Date

■ Each measuring cup below equals 1 cup. Trace the number of cups of liquid in the space provided.

①

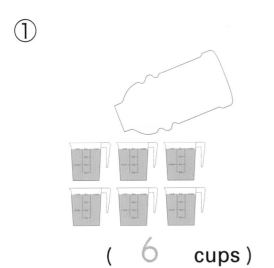

(6 cups)

②

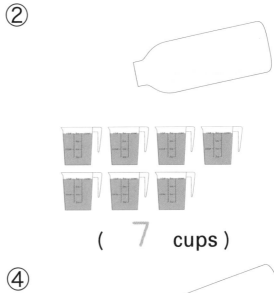

(7 cups)

③

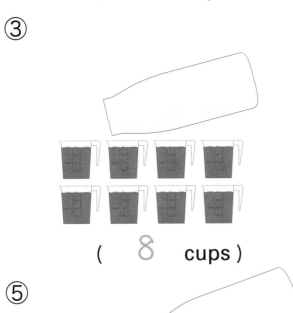

(8 cups)

④

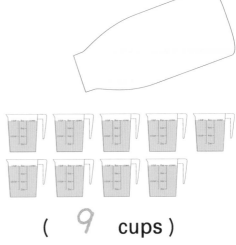

(9 cups)

⑤

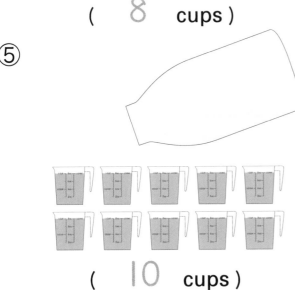

(10 cups)

35

■Each measuring cup below equals 1 cup. Write the number of cups of liquid in the space provided.

①

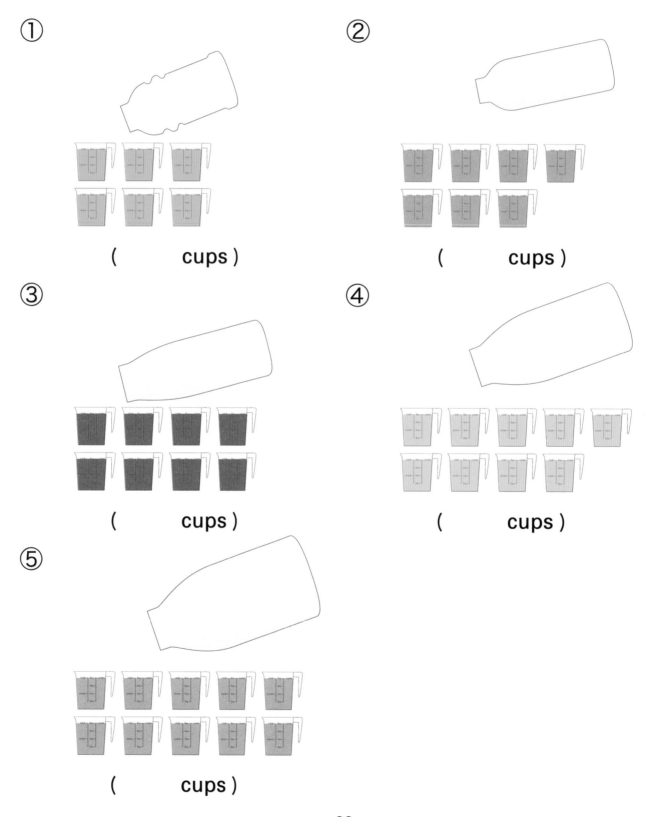

(cups)

②

(cups)

③

(cups)

④

(cups)

⑤

(cups)

 **Cups**

■ Each measuring cup below equals 1 cup. Write the number of cups of liquid in the space provided.

①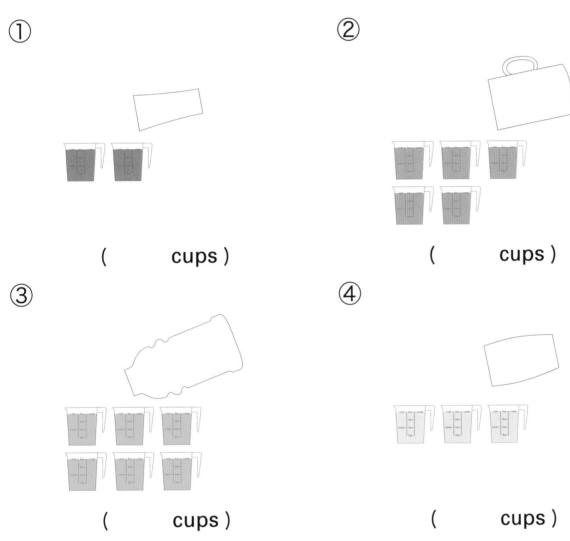

(cups)

②

(cups)

③

(cups)

④

(cups)

⑤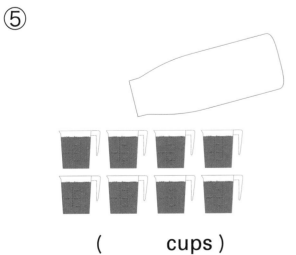

(cups)

37

■Each measuring cup below equals 1 cup. Write the number of cups of liquid in the space provided.

①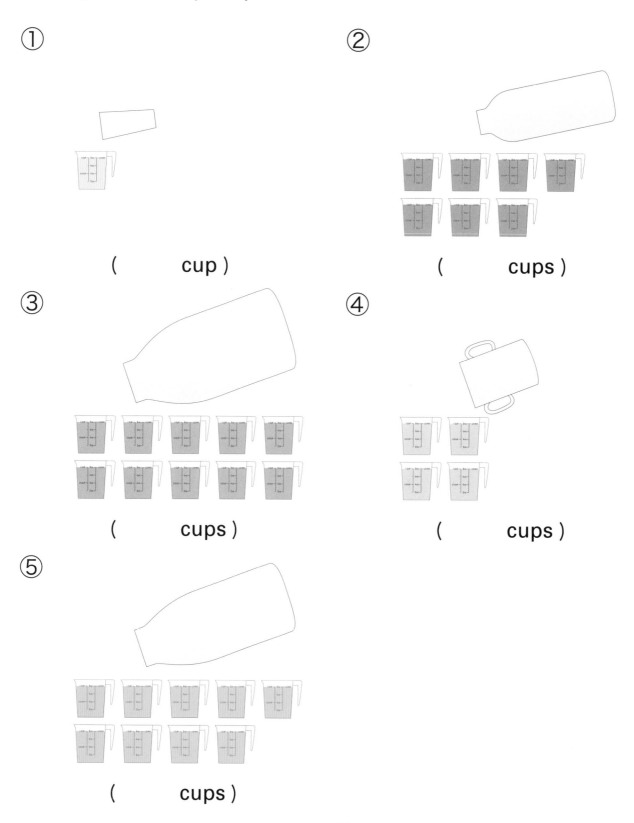

(cup)

②

(cups)

③

(cups)

④

(cups)

⑤

(cups)

 **Cups**

Name

Date

■ Each measuring cup below equals 1 cup. Write the number of cups of liquid in the space provided.

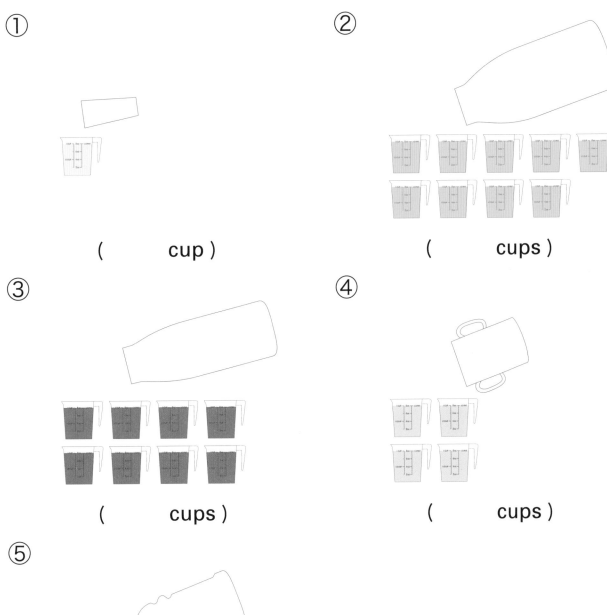

①   (cup)

②   (cups)

③   (cups)

④   (cups)

⑤   (cups)

■Each measuring cup below equals 1 cup. Write the number of cups of liquid in the space provided.

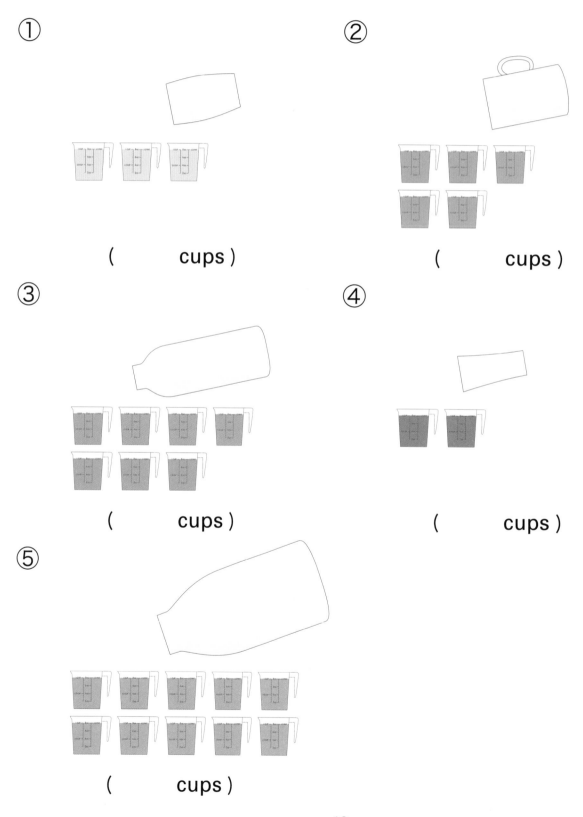

①

(cups)

②

(cups)

③

(cups)

④

(cups)

⑤

(cups)

Cups and Pints

■ Each measuring cup below equals 2 cups or 1 pint. Trace the volume of liquid in each measuring cup in the space provided.

①

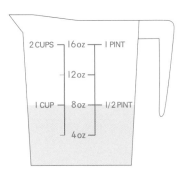

(1 c.)

②

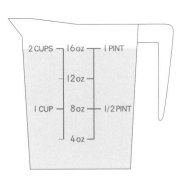

(2 c.)

③

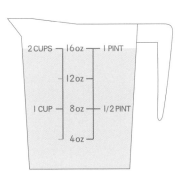

(1 pt.)

■Each measuring cup below equals 2 cups or 1 pint. Write the volume of liquid in each measuring cup in the space provided.

①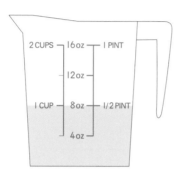

(c.)

②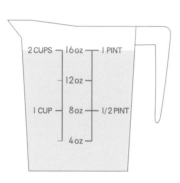

(c.)

③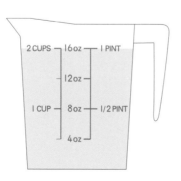

(pt.)

Cups and Pints

Name

Date

■ Each measuring cup below equals 2 cups or 1 pint. Write the volume of liquid in each measuring cup in the space provided.

①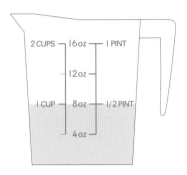

(c.)

②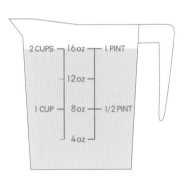

(pt.)

③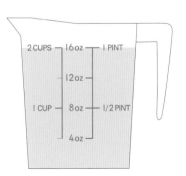

(c.)

■ Each measuring cup below equals 2 cups or 1 pint. Write the volume of liquid in each measuring cup in the space provided.

①

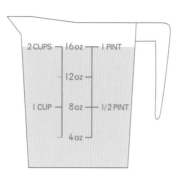

(c.)

②

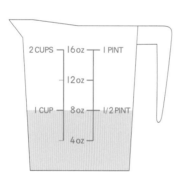

(c.)

③

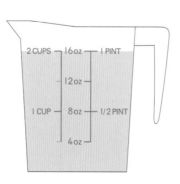

(pt.)

23 Cups and Pints

Name

Date

■ Each measuring cup below equals 2 cups or 1 pint. Trace the volume of liquid in the space provided.

①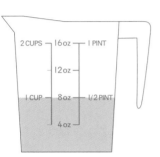

(1   c.)

②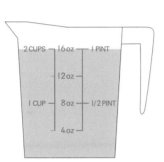

(2   c.) or (1   pt.)

③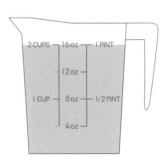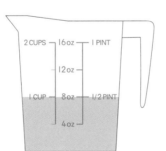

(1   pt.   1   c.)

④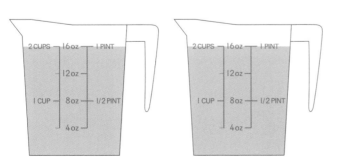

(2   pt.)

■Each measuring cup below equals 2 cups or 1 pint. Write the volume of liquid in the space provided.

①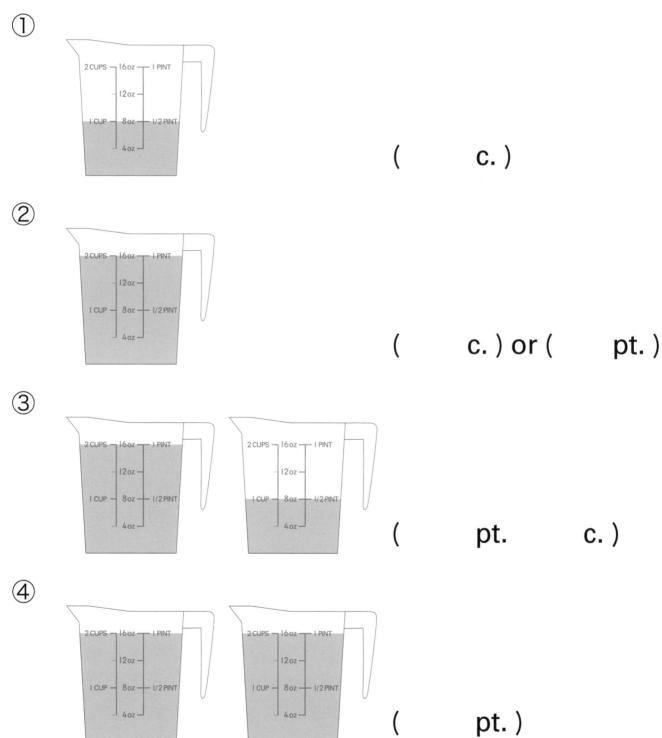

(c.)

②

(c.) or (pt.)

③

(pt.   c.)

④

(pt.)

24 Cups and Pints

Name

Date

■ Each measuring cup below equals 2 cups or 1 pint. Write the volume of liquid in the space provided.

①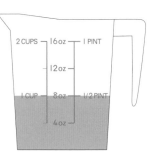

(c.)

②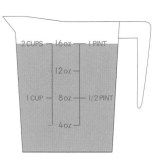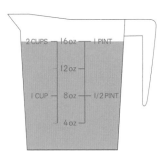

(pt.   c.)

③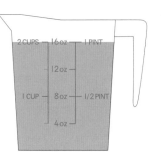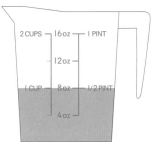

(pt.)

④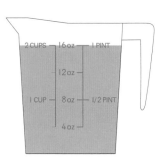

(pt.)

■ Each measuring cup below equals 2 cups or 1 pint. Write the volume of liquid in the space provided.

①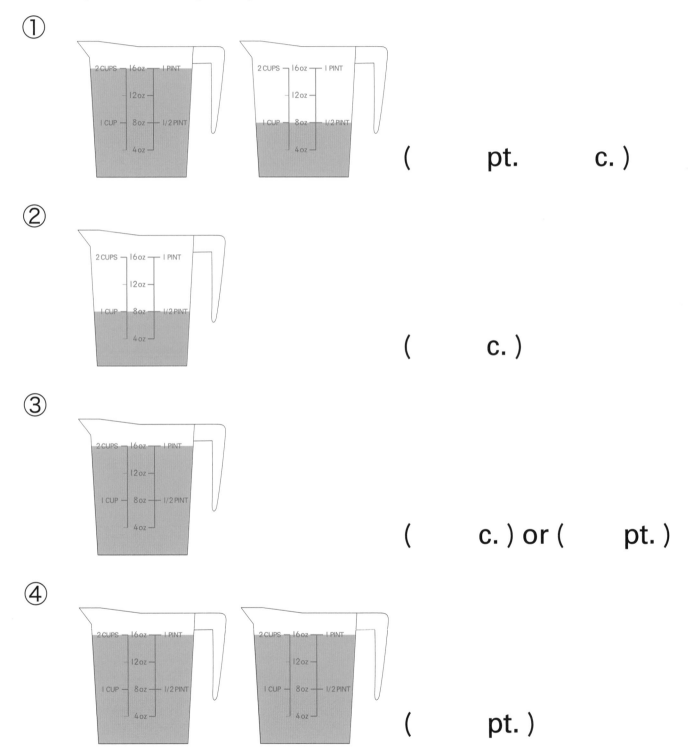

(pt.   c.)

②

(c.)

③

(c.) or (pt.)

④

(pt.)

■ Each measuring cup below equals 1 cup. Write the number of cups of liquid in the space provided.

①

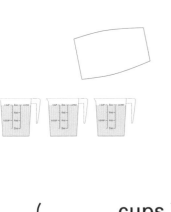

(cups)

②

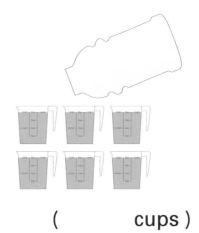

(cups)

③

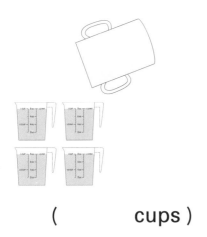

(cups)

④

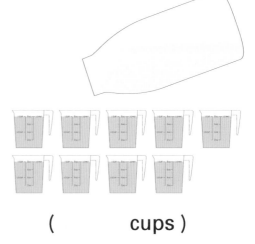

(cups)

⑤

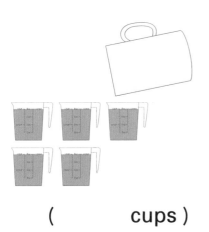

(cups)

■Each measuring cup below equals 2 cups or 1 pint. Write the volume of liquid in the space provided.

①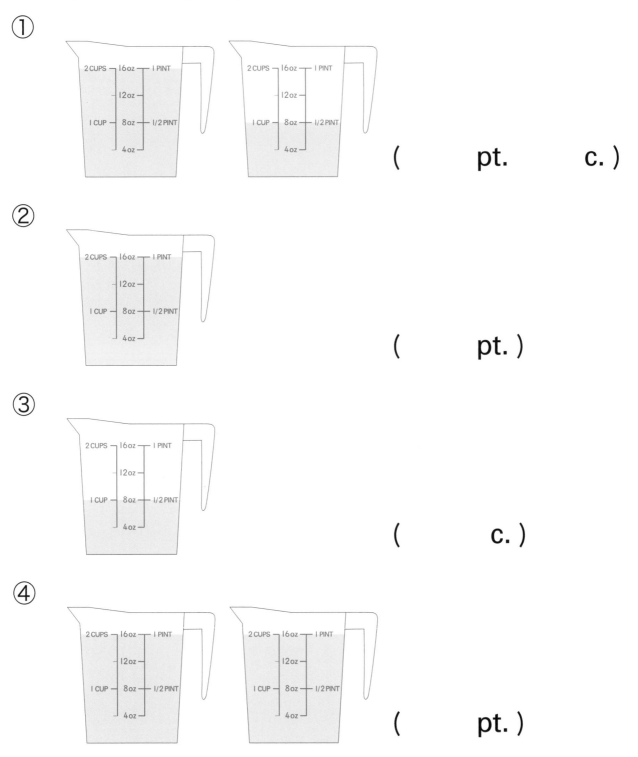

(pt.   c.)

②

(pt.)

③

(c.)

④

(pt.)

26 Liters

Name

Date

■ Each measuring cup below equals 1 liter. Trace the number of liters of liquid in the space provided.

①

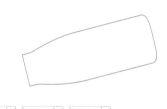

(1 liter)

②

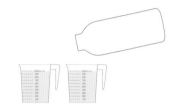

(2 liters)

③

(3 liters)

④

(4 liters)

⑤

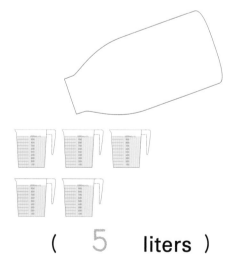

(5 liters)

■Each measuring cup below equals 1 liter. Write the number of liters of liquid in the space provided.

①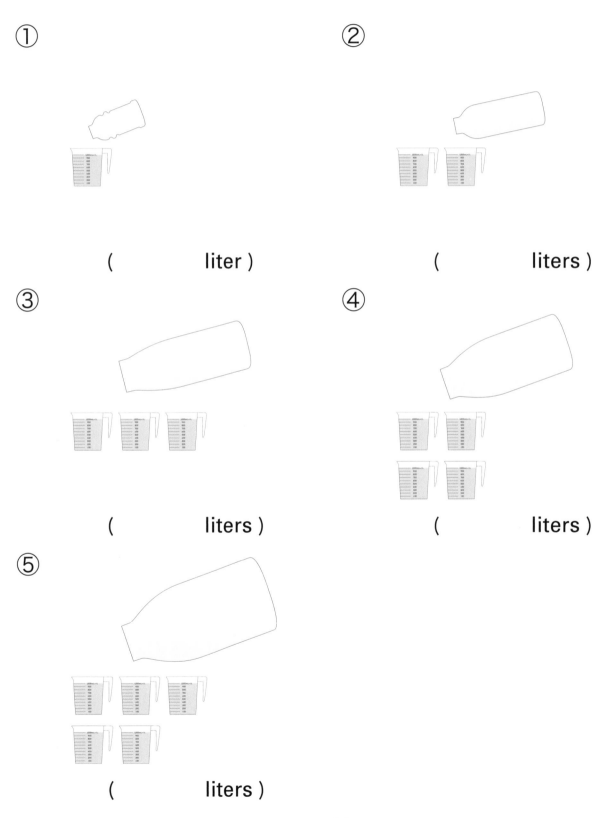

(liter)

②

(liters)

③

(liters)

④

(liters)

⑤

(liters)

27 Liters

■Each measuring cup below equals 1 liter. Trace the number of liters of liquid in the space provided.

①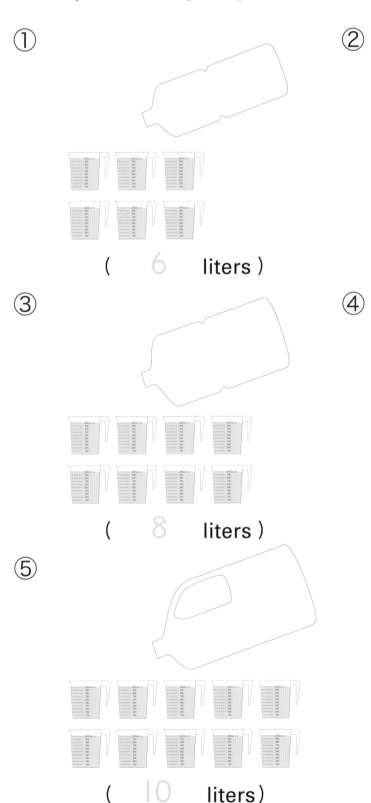

(6 liters)

②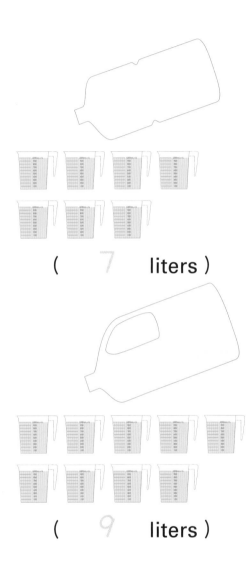

(7 liters)

③

(8 liters)

④

(9 liters)

⑤

(10 liters)

■ Each measuring cup below equals 1 liter. Write the number of liters of liquid in the space provided.

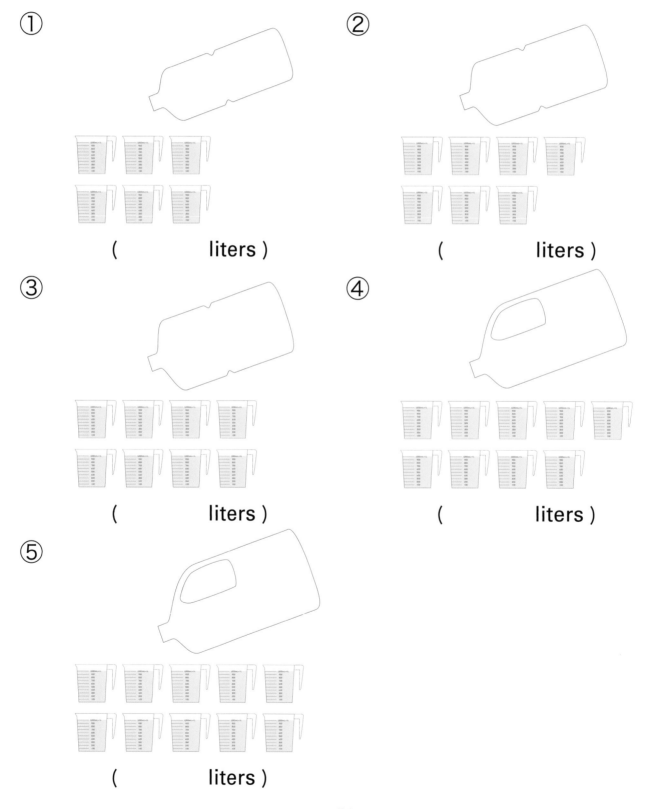

① (liters)

② (liters)

③ (liters)

④ (liters)

⑤ (liters)

Practicing Numbers 1 to 1,000

Name

Date

■ Trace each number while saying it aloud.

10	20	30	40	50	60	70	80	90	100
110	120	130	140	150	160	170	180	190	200
210	220	230	240	250	260	270	280	290	300
310	320	330	340	350	360	370	380	390	400
410	420	430	440	450	460	470	480	490	500
510	520	530	540	550	560	570	580	590	600
610	620	630	640	650	660	670	680	690	700
710	720	730	740	750	760	770	780	790	800
810	820	830	840	850	860	870	880	890	900
910	920	930	940	950	960	970	980	990	1,000

100	200	300	400	500	600	700	800	900	1,000

■Trace each number while saying it aloud.

10	20	30	40	50	60	70	80	90	100
110	120	130	140	150	160	170	180	190	200
210	220	230	240	250	260	270	280	290	300
310	320	330	340	350	360	370	380	390	400
410	420	430	440	450	460	470	480	490	500
510	520	530	540	550	560	570	580	590	600
610	620	630	640	650	660	670	680	690	700
710	720	730	740	750	760	770	780	790	800
810	820	830	840	850	860	870	880	890	900
910	920	930	940	950	960	970	980	990	1,000

100	200	300	400	500	600	700	800	900	1,000

29 Milliliters and Liters

Name

Date

■ Each measuring cup below equals 1,000 milliliters or 1 liter. Trace the volume of liquid in each measuring cup in the space provided.

①

(100　mL)

②

(200　mL)

③

(300　mL)

④

(400　mL)

⑤

(500　mL)

Each measuring cup below equals 1,000 milliliters or 1 liter. Write the volume of liquid in each measuring cup in the space provided.

①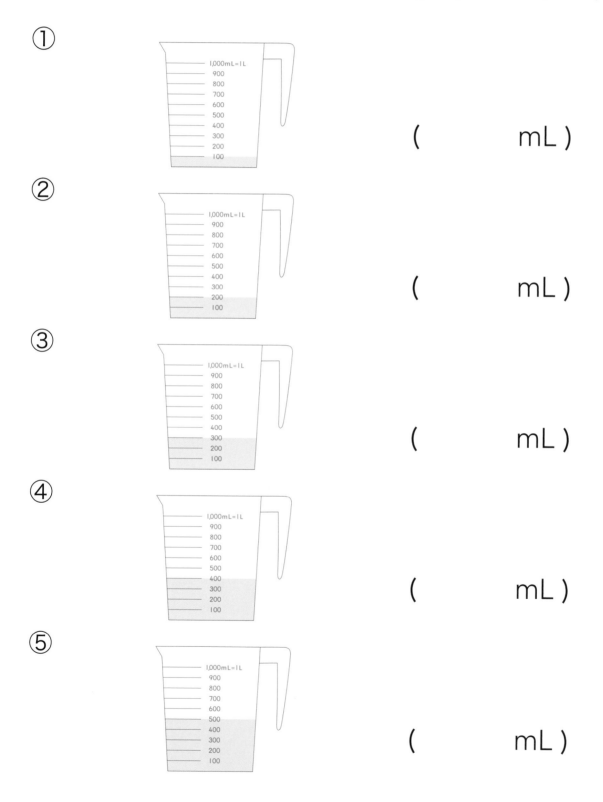

(mL)

②

(mL)

③

(mL)

④

(mL)

⑤

(mL)

■ Each measuring cup below equals 1,000 milliliters or 1 liter. Write the volume of liquid in each measuring cup in the space provided.

①

(600 mL)

②

(700 mL)

③

(800 mL)

④

(900 mL)

⑤

(1,000 mL) or (1 L)

■Each measuring cup below equals 1,000 milliliters or 1 liter. Write the volume of liquid in each measuring cup in the space provided.

①

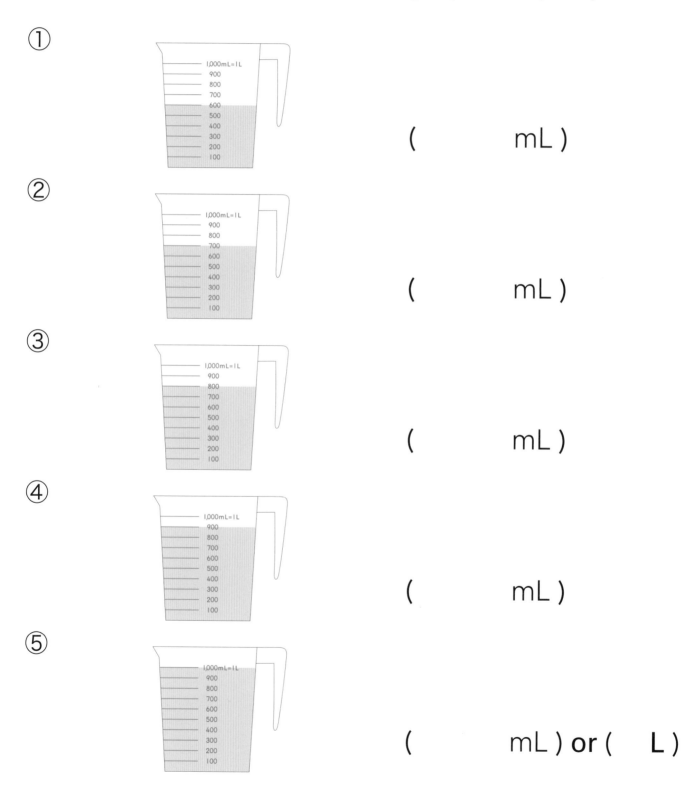

(mL)

②

(mL)

③

(mL)

④

(mL)

⑤

(mL) or (L)

31 Milliliters and Liters

Name

Date

■ Each measuring cup below equals 1,000 milliliters or 1 liter. Write the volume of liquid in each measuring cup in the space provided.

① (mL)

② (mL)

③ (mL)

④ (mL)

⑤ (mL)

⑥ (mL)

⑦ (mL)

⑧ (mL)
or
(L)

⑨ (mL)

⑩ (mL)

■Each measuring cup below equals 1,000 milliliters or 1 liter. Write
the volume of liquid in each measuring cup in the space provided.

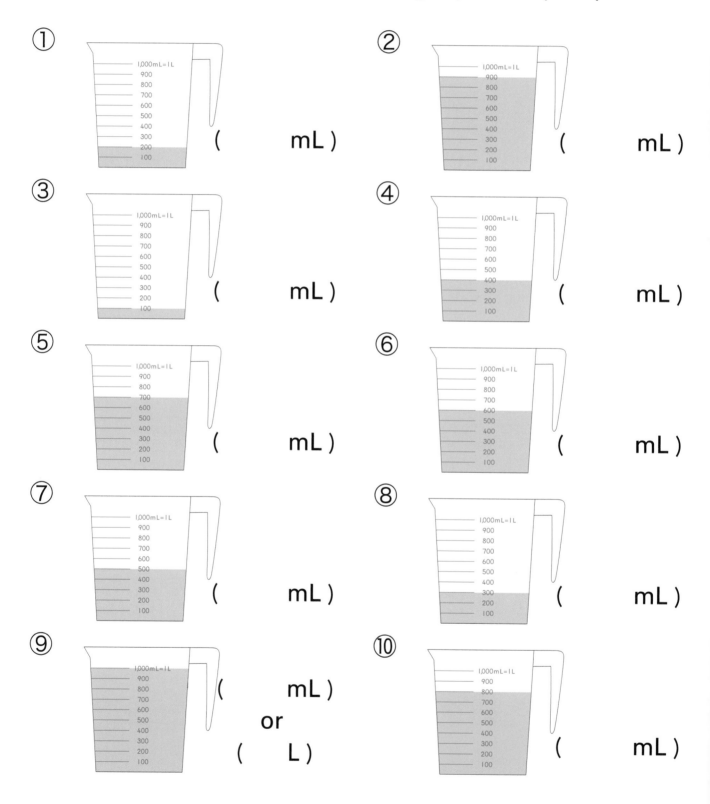

① (mL)

② (mL)

③ (mL)

④ (mL)

⑤ (mL)

⑥ (mL)

⑦ (mL)

⑧ (mL)

⑨ (mL)
   or
   (L)

⑩ (mL)

Name

Date

■Each measuring cup below equals 1,000 milliliters or 1 liter. Write the volume of liquid in each measuring cup in the space provided.

① 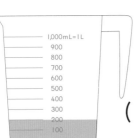 (mL)

② 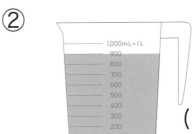 (mL)

③ 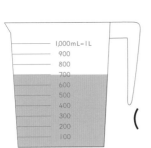 (mL)

④ 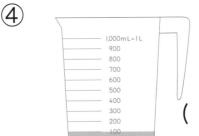 (mL)

⑤ 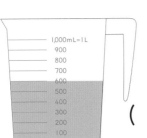 (mL)

⑥ 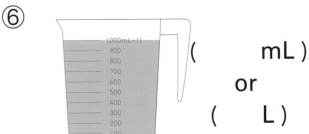 (mL)

or

(L)

⑦ 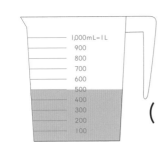 (mL)

⑧  (mL)

⑨ 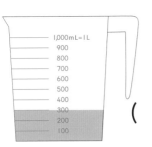 (mL)

⑩ 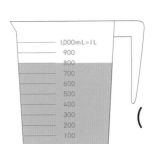 (mL)

■Each measuring cup below equals 1,000 milliliters or 1 liter. Write the volume of liquid in each measuring cup in the space provided.

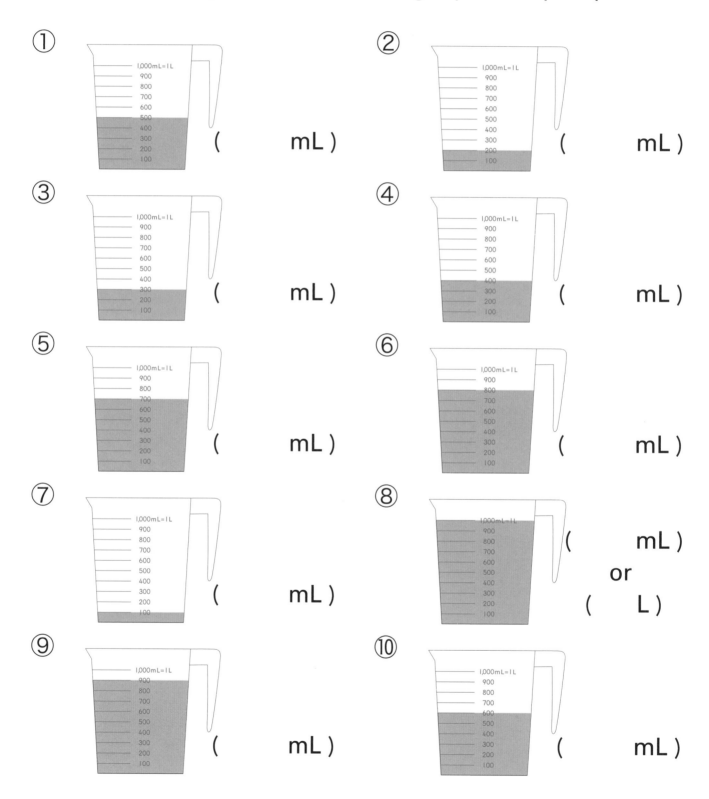

① (mL)

② (mL)

③ (mL)

④ (mL)

⑤ (mL)

⑥ (mL)

⑦ (mL)

⑧ (mL)
or
(L)

⑨ (mL)

⑩ (mL)

33 Milliliters and Liters

Name
Date

■Each bottle below equals 1,000 milliliters or 1 liter. Trace the volume of liquid in the space provided.

①

(1,000 mL)
or
(1 L)

②

(2,000 mL)
or
(2 L)

③

(3,000 mL)
or
(3 L)

④

(4,000 mL)
or
(4 L)

⑤

(5,000 mL)
or
(5 L)

■Each bottle below equals 1,000 milliliters or 1 liter. Write the volume of liquid in the space provided.

①

(mL)
or
(L)

②

(mL)
or
(L)

③

(mL)
or
(L)

④

(mL)
or
(L)

⑤

(mL)
or
(L)

Milliliters and Liters

■ Each bottle below equals 1,000 milliliters or 1 liter. Trace the volume of liquid in the space provided.

①

(6,000 mL)
or
(6 L)

②

(7,000 mL)
or
(7 L)

③

(8,000 mL)
or
(8 L)

④

(9,000 mL)
or
(9 L)

⑤

(10,000 mL)
or
(10 L)

■Each bottle below equals 1,000 milliliters or 1 liter. Write the volume
of liquid in the space provided.

①

(mL)
or
(L)

②

(mL)
or
(L)

③

(mL)
or
(L)

④

(mL)
or
(L)

⑤

(mL)
or
(L)

35 Milliliters and Liters

Name

Date

■ Each bottle below equals 1,000 milliliters or 1 liter. Write the volume of liquid in the space provided.

①

(mL)
or
(L)

②

(mL)
or
(L)

③

(mL)
or
(L)

④

(mL)
or
(L)

⑤

(mL)
or
(L)

■Each bottle below equals 1,000 milliliters or 1 liter. Write the volume of liquid in the space provided.

①

(mL)
or
(L)

②

(mL)
or
(L)

③

(mL)
or
(L)

④

(mL)
or
(L)

⑤

(mL)
or
(L)

36 Milliliters and Liters

Name

Date

■ Each bottle below equals 1,000 milliliters or 1 liter. Write the volume of liquid in the space provided.

①

(mL)
or
(L)

②

(mL)
or
(L)

③

(mL)
or
(L)

④

(mL)
or
(L)

⑤

(mL)
or
(L)

■Each bottle below equals 1,000 milliliters or 1 liter. Write the volume of liquid in the space provided.

①

(　　　mL)
or
(　L)

②

(　　　mL)
or
(　L)

③

(　　　mL)
or
(　L)

④

(　　　mL)
or
(　L)

⑤

(　　　mL)
or
(　L)

Review
Milliliters and Liters

■ Each measuring cup below equals 1,000 milliliters or 1 liter. Write the volume of liquid in each measuring cup in the space provided.

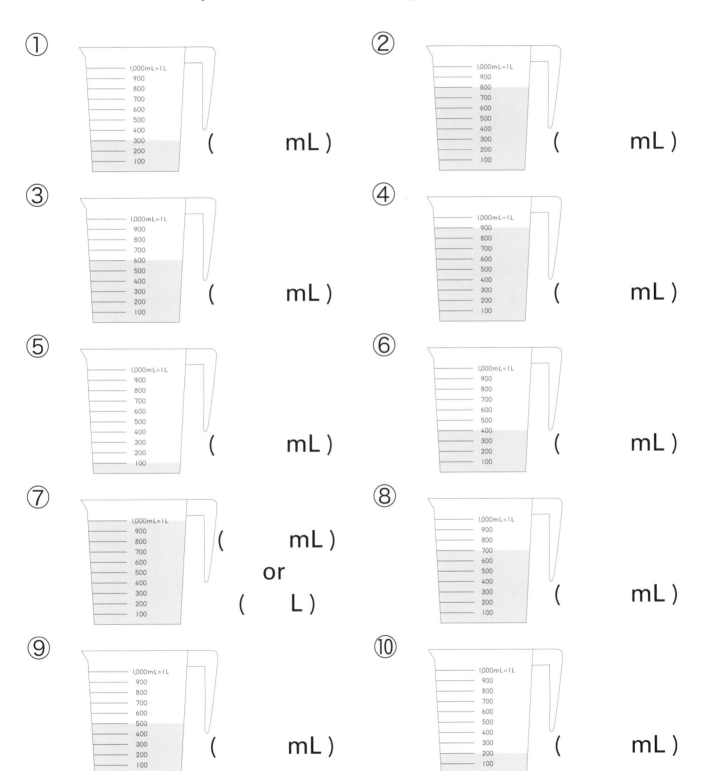

① (mL)

② (mL)

③ (mL)

④ (mL)

⑤ (mL)

⑥ (mL)

⑦ (mL)
or
(L)

⑧ (mL)

⑨ (mL)

⑩ (mL)

73

■Each bottle below equals 1,000 milliliters or 1 liter. Write the volume of liquid in the space provided.

①

(mL)
or
(L)

②

(mL)
or
(L)

③

(mL)
or
(L)

④

(mL)
or
(L)

⑤

(mL)
or
(L)

Name	
Date	

■ Each measuring cup below equals 2 cups or 1 pint. Write the volume of liquid in the space provided.

①

(pt.)

②

(c.)

③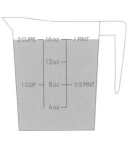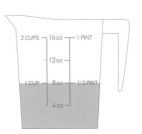

(pt.   c.)

④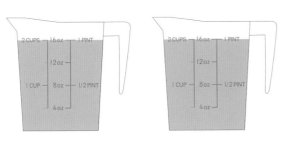

(pt.)

■Each bottle below equals 1,000 milliliters or 1 liter. Write the volume of liquid in the space provided.

①

(mL)
or
(L)

②

(mL)
or
(L)

③

(mL)
or
(L)

④

(mL)
or
(L)

⑤

(mL)
or
(L)

Name
Date

■Each measuring cup below equals 1 cup. Write the number of cups of liquid in the space provided.

①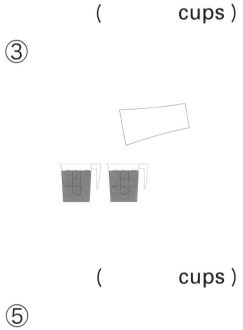

(cups)

②

(cups)

③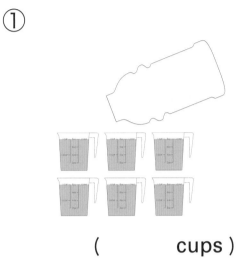

(cups)

④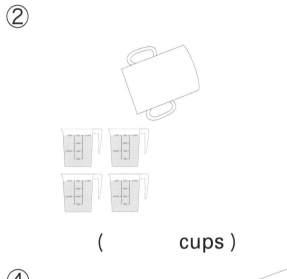

(cups)

⑤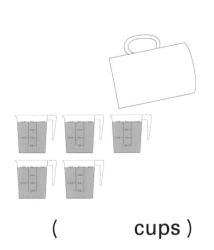

(cups)

■Each measuring cup below equals 1,000 milliliters or 1 liter. Write the volume of liquid in each measuring cup in the space provided.

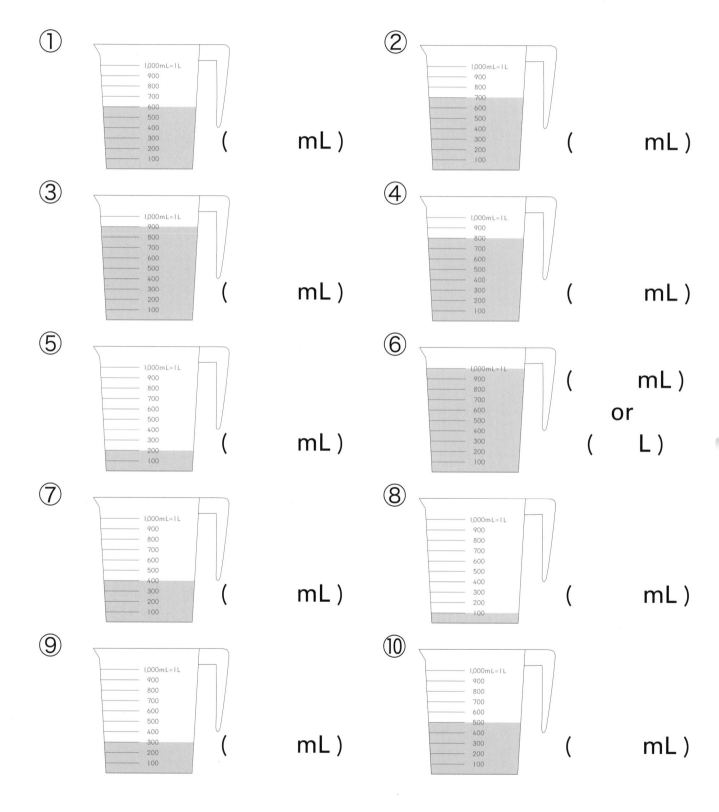

① (mL)

② (mL)

③ (mL)

④ (mL)

⑤ (mL)

⑥ (mL)
or
(L)

⑦ (mL)

⑧ (mL)

⑨ (mL)

⑩ (mL)

KUMON

Certificate of Achievement

is hereby congratulated on completing

My Book of Measurement: Volume

Presented on _____ , 20____

_____
Parent or Guardian